# PUERTO VALLARTA INSID

A Puerto Vallarta Travel Guide f(
Travelers

By Scott & Cathryn Arnell



ISBN: 978-0-9600263-3-3

2443 Fillmore Street #9115-380
San Francisco, California 94115

## Advance Praise for PV Insider

World travelers and close friends, Cathryn and Scott Arnell deliver a fabulous Insider's Guide to Puerto Vallarta for the discerning upscale traveler filled with everything you need to know to enjoy your stay in Puerto Vallarta. This guide is chock full of accurate and valuable information that will ensure you are "in the know" and will save you significant time and money during your stay.

*Stewart Haverlack*
*PV resident 2004–2014*
*Owner, Zumo Restaurant & Villa Limon Hotel Boutique, San Miguel de Allende, Guanajuato*
*Former Owner/Operator El Dorado Restaurant & Beach Club*

My wife and I have made Puerto Vallarta our second home for the past nine years. Cathryn and Scott have captured the very best of what this beautiful city has to offer and have reminded me that there are yet more things to experience in this paradise.

*Pat Ryan*
*Residents, Conchas Chinas, Puerto Vallarta*

As a Canadian having served the Puerto Vallarta real estate community for over 25 years, I've observed the constantly evolving landscape of this beautiful oceanside city, both literally and figuratively. Scott and Cathryn have clearly done so as well and captured its finest experiences, sport, dining, shopping, and other attractions for luxury travelers. Bravo for publishing a one-of-a-kind guide to this lovely community.

*David Pullen*
*David Pullen Properties*
*www.davidpullenproperties.com*

As a long-time pastor and wife serving the English-speaking community in Puerto Vallarta, we get to view all sides of life here. PV Insider focuses on the finer side of PV's life, providing Scott and Cathryn's personal views on favorite dining establishments, activities, and shopping, but also documenting practical information for both the luxury traveler and everyday visitor. We love the personal take on the establishments noted and that both extravagant and simple, relaxing venues are featured. Looking forward to next year's additions.

*Rick and Joy Lehman*
*Paradise Church*
*www.paradisechurchpv.org*

# PUERTO VALLARTA INSIDER

A Puerto Vallarta Travel Guide for
Villa Renters and Luxury Travelers

Tired of being misled by advertising and unreliable reviews? Learn from world travelers who have maintained a villa residence in Puerto Vallarta for over a decade.

## Disclaimer

We have written this book to recommend places to see, visit, dine at, and enjoy while in Puerto Vallarta. These recommendations are based solely on our own experiences during our time living in this wonderful place. But of course, we cannot guarantee everyone will appreciate Puerto Vallarta as much as we have.

We are not responsible and do not accept any liability for any negative experience you may have at any of the establishments mentioned in this book. And while we have made every effort to ensure the information included in this book is accurate, Puerto Vallarta evolves and changes every day, so details, pricing, etc. may not reflect what you encounter upon a visit.

## Free Bonus with Every Purchase

*Puerto Vallarta Insider* has been written for travelers who are planning a dream holiday in the beautiful coastal city of Puerto Vallarta and will rent (or perhaps have already rented) a luxury villa for their stay. For this reason, the book does not address lodging in the city or make any recommendations on this topic.

If you have not yet found the perfect villa for your holiday, as a small token of thanks for buying this book, we'd like to send you a bonus e-book—at No Extra Charge.

Written by ourselves, the authors of *Puerto Vallarta Insider*, the e-book, *Holiday Bliss: Finding The Perfect Luxury Villa To Rent For Your Holiday,* identifies the process involved in finding the ideal vacation villa. It's a process we have used on our own travels around the world to identify luxury accommodations that help make our holidays all the more unforgettable.

If you'd like to receive this bonus e-book, go to
https://puertovallartaluxuryvilla.com/holiday-bliss-download/
to download your complimentary copy now.

Puerto Vallarta is one of the most beautiful cities on Mexico's Pacific coast, and we hope that *Puerto Vallarta Insider* helps to make your stay in our favorite city extra special. *¡Hasta pronto!*

Table of Contents

## "Where do locals like us go?"

That's what we always ask ourselves whenever we're away from home, which we are nearly every week. We're a married couple who both work in international finance on multiple continents, traveling 60%–70% of the time for the last 30 years.

For some time now, while we're not in one of our homes in Mexico, The Netherlands, or Switzerland, we have rented villas when taking time off, instead of staying at hotels. We spend so much of our work life in hotels, the last thing we want to do when we're on holiday is to check into another. Sharing the pool with 50 of our "closest friends"; eating three room-service or restaurant meals a day; walking through anonymous lobbies—it's not exactly a home away from home!

Whether we're at one of our homes or on holiday in a rented villa, we normally don't go out much as we usually reserve a home with a great view or ambience, often with a chef that serves dinner whenever we choose. In fact, we usually only go to restaurants or sights if we're meeting local friends or if one has recommended the location. That way, we know we're going to a place that's worthwhile, somewhere that is known for a consistently fine experience, be it a restaurant or an adventure. We live in a number of locations popular with tourists, and the places we like aren't always the places that tourists frequent.

So, we always want to know, "Where do locals *like us* go?" And if you're reading this, you're probably contemplating (or maybe have already booked) a vacation villa in Puerto Vallarta and want to know the same thing. If so, this guide is for you.

Puerto Vallarta is one of the world's most beautiful places. We ended up buying an undeveloped plot of land and built our villa, *Casa Dos Cisnes (www.pvluxuryvilla.com)*, because whenever we had time free in North America, we kept coming back to Puerto Vallarta. In creating a life here over the years, we've learned about, and enjoyed first-hand, some of the best places to go and things to do.

*The Rotunda by the Sea* by Alejandro Colunga, along the Malecón, Puerto Vallarta. Photo by Another Believer.

A key aspect of planning the perfect vacation getaway is choosing what to do when you get there. As Mexico's second-largest tourist destination, Puerto Vallarta is blessed with an amazing array of options, but the quality can vary greatly. We have written *Puerto Vallarta Insider* to filter out the noise that other general tourist guidebooks and tourist propaganda contain, to help make your vacation planning easier. In it, we share the few places we go to when we go out and tell you about what to expect and why we like it.

When you rent a villa, your desires are more discerning, and your needs are completely different from someone booking a hotel or resort stay. You will generally be looking for more privacy, you will have a full staff with a chef (if you don't, change your villa!) and your need to venture out is greatly reduced. So, each time you do, you'll want to make the experience count.

We have curated just the essential information for discerning luxury travelers. The restaurants and services we present here are ones we personally know, have patronized over the years when in residence in Puerto Vallarta, and consider reliable because they have stood the test of time. In many cases, we have established agreements specifically for our guests staying at *Casa Dos Cisnes* to receive VIP treatment because of our confidence in the establishment.

We hope that, with this guide, you'll spend less time planning your holiday and more time **on** holiday. After all, holidays should be about relaxing and not adding to your "to do" tasks.

And although we mention the "luxury traveler," we believe that the "good life" we describe is available to anyone who desires a certain standard of food and accommodation. It's all about how you want to live your life, not the price.

Scott & Cathryn Arnell

Puerto Vallarta, Jalisco, Mexico

December 2018

## About Puerto Vallarta

As we mentioned earlier, Puerto Vallarta is Mexico's second-largest tourist destination. Since it overlooks the beautiful Banderas Bay (*Bahía de Banderas*), its popularity is not surprising, and it has grown to a population of just over 255,000 residents, making it the fifth-largest city in the State of Jalisco.

But those are just basic statistics. It has also been described as "*La Ciudad más Amigable del Mundo*" (The Friendliest City in the World), and despite the growth of tourist resorts, we find that it pretty much continues to live up to that reputation.

It's famed for a slower, more peaceful pace of life, for its sandy beaches and clear blue waters, and for cool tropical breezes and lush palm-covered mountains. Unlike some of Mexico's other resort destinations (such as Ixtapa, Acapulco, and Cancún), Puerto Vallarta has retained its own sense of identity and has not completely sold out to Spring Break madness, managing to embrace tourism without sacrificing its historical roots.

### Weather

It's been said that the Puerto Vallarta region is in "perpetual summer," and that's not an unfair assessment. In general, temperatures range from 62°F–90°F (16°C–32°C), but tropical winds off the Pacific and summer rains help to maintain a pleasant environment.

In late spring and summer, which is considered the low season, daytime temperatures can get quite high. The air gets progressively more humid over the course of the season, and rain and thunderstorms are common, particularly in the afternoons. May is often the warmest and driest month (88°F/31°C) and, from July through September, expect temperatures in the high 80s to low 90s (30°C–34°C) but with substantial humidity.

Up in the hills of Conchas Chinas (where our villa, *Casa Dos Cisnes* is located), the temperatures are usually a few degrees lower and there's almost always a breeze coming up the hills from the sea, which balances the sometimes-stifling heat that you will experience in the flatter areas of the bay. The tropical storms that visit in the afternoon and evenings can bring heavy rains with thunder and amazing streaks of lightning over the bay, which is mesmerizing to watch, especially from a high vantage point.

This season is also the best time for water activities like morning diving and snorkeling when the ocean is still calm. The lower "*gringo*" tourist population means the town is more relaxed and reservations at even the most popular restaurants are easily obtained (but check to make sure your choice of restaurant is open, as this is also a popular time for Mexican nationals from Guadalajara and Mexico City to take their school summer holiday vacations).

In late fall and winter, daytime temperatures stay around a perfect high of 80°F–85°F (27°C–30°C), dropping to 60°F–65°F (16°C–18°C) by midnight with very low humidity. This is the "high season," when northerners flee the cold weather of the US and Canada for a place where the forecast is nearly the same every day (sunny with clear skies!) from December through April.

*Vallarta Dancers* by Jim Demetro along the Malecón, Puerto Vallarta. Photo by Another Believer.

## Orientation

When you're looking for a villa to rent, agents and online rental sites present villas in Mismaloya, Amapas, Nuevo Vallarta and Punta de Mita all as being "Puerto Vallarta." In fact, these geographical locations are vastly different, and quite far apart, so make sure to consider this when deciding where to reside, even if only for a holiday. But for us, there was a clear reason why we chose to live in Conchas Chinas.

For the most intimate experience of Puerto Vallarta, we prefer to be within five minutes or so of the Downtown area, where you're within walking distance of the colorful Old Town sights, cafés, restaurants, and shops. Conchas Chinas puts you within easy reach of the city's best restaurants and nightlife, close to the beach and bay, yet away from the hustle and bustle that comes with tourist life.

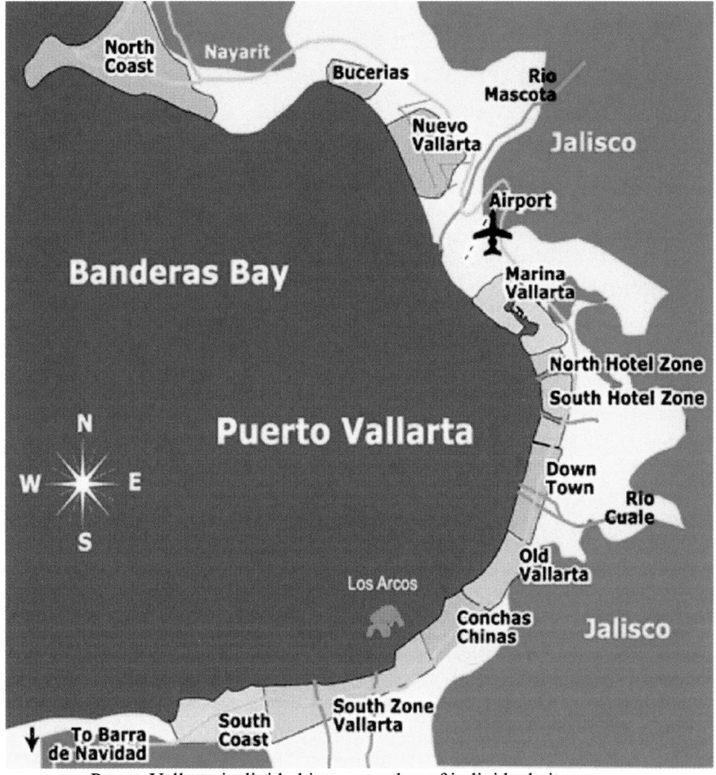

Puerto Vallarta is divided into a number of individual city zones.

To help you get an accurate picture, we've divided the city into three areas: Downtown, North of Downtown and South of Downtown.

**Downtown**

The heart of Puerto Vallarta remains Old Town where you'll find the Malecón, a long winding promenade along the shoreline which crosses Río Cuale (the River Cuale, which divides the town) to provide the only walking route to link the areas north and south of the river. It's filled with street food and live entertainment, from living statues to musicians, and is a favorite location from which to watch the sunset.

**El Centro (Downtown)** – Set on the north side of Río Cuale, El Centro rises abruptly from the sea with its hilly, cobblestone streets lined with white-washed homes and shops. It's only a 10-minute drive from *Casa Dos Cisnes*, depending on what time you set off on your journey.

**Zona Romántica (Romantic Zone)** – Set on the south side of the river, Zona Romántica has Puerto Vallarta's highest density of restaurants and boutique shops. *Casa Dos Cisnes* is literally a five-minute drive away. This area is one of our favorite parts of town but is in the process of undergoing significant transformation with several new condominium buildings under construction. The bar scene can be amazingly noisy at night, but we appreciate the fast access to some of the town's great restaurants and clubs, as well as the ability to quickly retreat to the quiet of our villa.

We often park our car and jog (or walk) on the Malecón from here in the mornings. Our reward is picking up fresh *croissants aux amandes* (almond croissants) at Eric's Paris Café (Pino Suarez 158, Basilio Badillo 162 | (322) 222-8472 | 8am–8pm Mon–Sat, high season only) about a block off the Malecón to take back home for breakfast.

We live in Europe most of the year and have easy access to fresh French bakeries daily, but Eric's croissants transcend even the most decadent we get in Europe.

## South of Downtown

On the southern edge of the city, just behind Los Muertos Beach, are the upscale residential neighborhoods of Amapas and Conchas Chinas, the latter where *Casa Dos Cisnes* is located. But there is a difference:

> **Amapas** – Although closer to Downtown Puerto Vallarta, Amapas is a heavily developed residential area; one we consider to have too many large condo buildings, too close together. There are, however, stunning views from here.
>
> **Conchas Chinas** – We chose Conchas Chinas, not because it's known as the "Beverly Hills of Puerto Vallarta" (although it is!), but because of its sense of community, with many long-time residents who appreciate the neighborhood and each other. That, in combination with its proximity to town, multiple homes built in a Colonial Mexican style, spectacular views of the entire bay, and backdrops of jungle hillsides with indigenous flora and fauna made it a compelling choice for us.

The sun sets into Banderas Bay, Conchas Chinas Beach, Puerto Vallarta. Photo by Daryl Mitchell

What both residential areas share is Highway 200, easy access to wonderful white beaches of the bay, and arguably the best panoramic views of the Pacific. The beaches to the west of the highway are an explorer's dream, dotted with boulders and carved with coves and rocky grottos. On the east side of the highway, the residential areas on the hillside provide incredible observation points. From Conchas Chinas, there are two exits that put you directly on the highway, with north heading into town and south to the beaches and ocean-side communities.

South of Conchas Chinas are the areas of Punta Negra, Garza Blanca, and Sierra del Mar, before the town of Mismaloya. All of these areas boast similarly impressive ocean views and lush hillside vegetation, but they are also quite a distance from Downtown Puerto Vallarta. Mismaloya, for example, is a 30-minute drive from the city, a commute that is getting longer because of continued development drawing more car and truck traffic.

### North of Downtown

The areas north of Downtown are much less picturesque, and quite a distance from the restaurants and shopping in town. But it is closest to the airport, and if you enjoy golfing or boating, then this is an area you are likely to spend some time in.

> **Zona Hotelera (Hotel Zone)** – A very busy avenue, with malls, businesses, high-rise hotels, and no charm whatsoever, although most hotels have direct access to the beach.
>
> **Marina Vallarta** – Populated by shopping centers and deluxe hotels squeezed between a golf course and the city's main yacht marina, with a large, flat residential section resembling an American subdivision. There are ocean views from some high-rise apartments and beach hotels but there is little vegetation, and there is no view at night unless you face the town. Thanks to the lack of a hillside location, the air is stagnant in the warm months of late spring to late fall, and the airport neighbors the marina. The location is convenient, however, if you intend to spend a significant time golfing, boating, or fishing.

**Nuevo Vallarta** – An area populated mainly by golf courses, exclusive condos, and luxurious restaurants, it has the second-highest number of hotels in the country. Many of the villas and condos are directly on the golf course. The area is very flat and, unless you're on the beach, it has no views. Again, the lack of a hillside location means the air can be stagnant, forcing you into air-conditioned quarters for relief from the heat. Access to Downtown takes at least 30 minutes.

**Riviera Nayarit** – Has pristine beaches, luxurious resorts, and dozens of laid-back towns loved by artists, surfers, and celebrities. But it's a good 45 to 60-minute drive north from the airport, depending on where you're going, and then another 20 minutes to get to a restaurant in Downtown Puerto Vallarta. If you choose to vacation here, you should be seeking a retreat from civilization, and a very casual (think "hippie-like") atmosphere.

**Punta de Mita** – The farthest point of Banderas Bay, and loved by jet-setters and the famous for luxury, get-away-from-it-all vacations. It's probably the best place for aquatic activities, with almost every seafront restaurant offering rental services and classes. It's also the main departure point for a lot of whale-watching excursions in the winter or boats to the Marietas Islands. Lots of luxury restaurants, but you'll need a reservation to access the primary Four Seasons resort.

It's not the place if you're looking to settle in for a while and be part of a community; an acquaintance of ours told us that the Punta de Mita development has only eight full-time expatriate residents. Nor should you target the area if you're looking for quality **and** reasonable cost; accommodations, restaurants, and activities all carry 5-Star prices.

## Getting to Puerto Vallarta

Puerto Vallarta's international airport (Gustavo Díaz Ordáz Airport, or PVR) is 4 miles (7 km) north of Downtown. It's small but busy practically all year round, with more than 4 million passengers passing through.

There are non-stop flights on major airlines from several major US and Canadian cities, but many more with stopovers in Mexico City. In many cases, the stopover results in the entire trip taking the better part of a day, so we don't recommend it unless absolutely necessary. For the latest non-stop flights into Puerto Vallarta's airport, go to www.aeropuertosgap.com.mx/en/puerto-vallarta-3.html.
Flying times are about: 2.5 hours from Houston; 3 hours from Los Angeles; 3.5 hours from Denver and San Francisco; 5.5 hours from Edmonton, Montreal, and Quebec; 6 hours from Toronto, and Vancouver; and around 8 hours from New York.

## Getting Around

Puerto Vallarta has no local train or urban rail system, so getting around is limited to public bus, rental cars, taxis, or Uber (which started services in PV in 2017). Bus transport is plentiful, but for people renting villas, we don't recommend it unless you want a "developing country" experience. The money saved isn't worth the hassle and it's unlikely that your villa is on a bus line (if it is, you probably should change your villa!)

Renting a car is not usually necessary, unless you plan on taking a lot of day trips out of town. Besides, traffic can be high, and parking is difficult in town unless you park in the large, pay-by-the-hour public parking garages available at either end of town. We do rent a car when we're in residence in order to go to the coiffure, meet friends etc. But most days, it sits in the garage and doesn't move.

If you do rent a car, stick with the major rental companies to avoid game-playing with the supplemental insurance. Briefly, the myriad car rental companies with names you don't recognize advertise online with amazingly cheap daily rates. When you arrive, they will require you to purchase supplemental insurance at a daily rate that generally dwarfs the rental rate of the car. If you attempt to discuss, or show them your internet print-out etc., they will refuse to rent to you at which point you either pay or take a cab to another company (all car rental companies are off the airport premises). Take our word, it's not an enjoyable way to start a relaxing vacation.

We always rent from Hertz because our status, due to constant business travel, provides certain benefits. Based on our research, their rates include the minimum insurance coverage required under Mexican law. Supplemental insurance is, of course, also offered. We imagine, but have never inquired, that Avis and the other major car rental companies are similar given their global presence. Prior to reserving a car, we would recommend that you do your own research given the above is not legal advice and may have changed since we completed our analysis.

The market on Isla Cuale in Puerto Vallarta.
Photo via: Garza Blanca

Taxis, on the other hand, are plentiful, can be hailed on the street and are inexpensive. All taxi rates are fixed rates based on defined zones of the town and there are no meters. Travel within a zone is about 50 pesos, a little under $3 based on current exchange rates, but once you cross a zone line, the cost increases. So, for example, from Downtown to Zona Hotelera, expect to pay about 80 pesos ($4.50), to Mismaloya around 130 pesos ($7). At the airport, you can get a taxi voucher at an official taxi kiosk. Expect to pay just over 200 pesos (US$11 at the time of writing) for a cab to Downtown.

It's advisable to make sure you ask what the full fare is, and that it roughly corresponds to what we've quoted above, before getting in the taxi to avoid any game playing at the destination. And make sure that the driver has change before getting in. Also, make a note of the taxi number in case you leave any objects behind.

Uber is relatively new in PV and is still experiencing some growing pains, particularly in the state of Nayarit. Uber is about 25%–50% cheaper than a taxi as of this writing. Its ability to access the airport may change over time, so check the app if this is your preferred method of transport.

If you want a private car, you can arrange to have one meet you at the airport. We use Superior Tours Vallarta (if you are dialing from the US or Canada: 011 52 322 222 0024).

**Festivals & Holidays**

Whenever you arrive in Puerto Vallarta, there is likely to be some kind of holiday or festival around the corner. Not just confined to Christmas and New Year, a host of religious holidays and local saint's days can result in packed beaches, jammed traffic, closed amenities, and street carnivals.

Below is a calendar list of national and notable Puerto Vallarta-region holidays and festivals. Some dates can vary from year to year, so you should check before you schedule your holiday.

**Jan 6**: *Día de los Reyes* (Day of the Kings), traditional gift exchange
**Feb 5**: Constitution Day, commemorating 1857 & 1917 constitutions (national holiday)
**Feb 24**: Flag Day (national holiday)

**Feb**: *Mardi Gras*, 4 days of celebrations ending on Ash Wednesday
**Feb 21–28**: Flower & Garden Festival at Vallarta Botanical Gardens
**Mar–Apr**: Electro Beach Puerto Vallarta, 42-day Electronic Dance Music festival
**Mar 21**: Birthday of Benito Juárez, the "Lincoln of Mexico" (national holiday)
**April**: *Semana Santa*, Holy Week, 7 days ending on Easter Sunday (national holiday)
**May 1**: Labor Day (national holiday)
**May 5**: *Cinco de Mayo*, defeat of the French at Puebla in 1862 (national holiday)
**May–June**: May Festival (municipality birthday with concerts, art exhibits, and parade)
**Sept 16**: Independence Day (national holiday)
**Oct 12**: *Día de la Raza*, like Columbus Day in US (national holiday)
**Nov 1**: *Día de Todos los Santos* (All Saints' Day), in honor of the souls of children
**Nov 2**: *Día de los Fieles Disfuntos* (Commonly referred to as Day of the Dead or *Dia de los Muertos* which actually refers to the entire celebration of October 31–November 2), in honor of ancestors
**Nov 20**: Revolution Day, anniversary of the 1910–1917 Revolution (national holiday)
**Dec 1–12**: *Día de Nuestra Señora de Guadalupe* (Festival of the Virgin of Guadalupe)
**Dec 16–24**: Christmas Week (week of *posadas* and *piñatas*)

## What to See

If you've chosen to come to Puerto Vallarta you're probably already familiar with the city's popular tourist destinations. But not everywhere is worth going to or seeing. We have spent enough time here to have learned the difference and have a shortlist of places we still enjoy visiting.

Puerto Vallarta's cathedral spire, the Church of Our Lady of Guadalupe. Photo by: Susie Albin-Najera

### The Malecón

This is Puerto Vallarta's seafront walkway, stretching for nearly a mile along the coastal edge of Downtown, starting at The Millennia Statue near the Hotel Rosita and ending at the amphitheater (Aquiles Serdán Plaza) beside the *zocalo*, which is called the Plaza de Armas.

A few years ago, after hurricane Kenna, the Malecón was extended south past the amphitheater to the Río Cuale (Cuale River) which is called the “New Malecón.” You can stroll all the way south to Los Muertos Beach by crossing a pedestrian bridge over the river and Isla Río Cuale (River Cuale Island).

It’s been a pedestrian zone since 2011, and since then, its popularity has grown even more. This is one of the nicest aspects of Puerto Vallarta and it’s unusual for a Mexican resort town to have preserved this much of the Downtown beach front for the public. We regularly go jogging here early in the morning, as it is a wonderfully long stretch to run on alongside the sea and impossible to imagine the dark, cold dreary days of Europe in the winter months from where we escaped.

Most people enjoy strolling along the Malecón, perusing the shops, snapping photos, and taking in the outstanding views of the Pacific. Many of the city’s most memorable sights are found along its route too, including some beautiful sculptures by both locally and nationally celebrated artists.

One of the best sights is the Church of Our Lady of Guadalupe, Puerto Vallarta’s iconic cathedral, at the south end of the esplanade. In front of the cathedral, across the Plaza de Armas, is Los Arcos Amphitheater (The Arches), a row of four picturesque arches against a backdrop of the bay. The smaller amphitheater nearby is a favorite spot for street performers.

Venders along the Malecon in Puerto Vallarta. Photo by Andrew Milligan Sumo

## Isla Río Cuale

Near the mouth of the Río Cuale is a sandy island, Isla Río Cuale. The island only appeared in the river mouth in the 1920s, but there are a number of pedestrian bridges linking it with Downtown and Zona Romántica, so it's popular for anyone who wants a quiet stroll away from the city. It has plenty of cafés, restaurants, and flea markets to occupy your time.

We recommend the Museo del Cuale, on the west end of the island. It's small but has some interesting archaeological exhibits detailing the pre-Hispanic history of the city and area. There is also the Mercado Municipal Río Cuale, a collection of stalls selling arts and crafts, and a little further on, you'll find John Huston Plaza, where there is a bronze statue of the Hollywood director, who spent time in Puerto Vallarta when making *Night Of The Iguana* in 1963. The Mercado is a great place to pick up souvenirs, purses, and resort clothes. However, the quality of these items can vary greatly, so take care when making a purchase. Bargaining is expected, and prices generally start quite high (compared with what they will ultimately accept).

**Zona Romántica**

Zona Romántica is the cultural hub of Puerta Vallarta and is lively all year round. It's filled with shops, art galleries, markets, cafés, bars, and restaurants, so it's great if you are a fan of exciting nightlife.

Basilio Badillo is the main thoroughfare, and it's where you'll find most of the activity. We enjoy the Farmers Market, the oldest in PV, which is held each morning at Lazaro Cárdenas Park (during high season only). You'll find everything there from freshly baked products and artisan foods to handmade clothing and jewelry.

Los Muertos Pier, Puerto Vallarta. Photo by Katalin Szarvas

The new Los Muertos Pier, which opened in 2013, is found at the end of Basilio Badillo. It stretches for 320 ft out into Banderas Bay, is colorfully lit in the evening, and while it can be a nice, romantic walk to take at night, it is also often quite crowded.

**Estero El Salado**

(Av Francisco Medina Ascencio S/N, Villa Las Flores| (322) 201-7361 | 9am–5pm Mon–Sat | www.esterodelsalado.org).

If you prefer getting a little closer to nature, we recommend visiting Estero El Salado. It's close to the airport, so it's a bit of a journey from where we live in Conchas Chinas, but a boat tour into the heart of the 168-hectare protected urban estuary is worth the effort.

There are hundreds of types of flora and fauna to view, including crocodiles, iguanas, and dozens of bird species. Boat tours run four times daily from Tuesday through Friday (9am, 11am, 1pm, 3pm), and three times (9am, 11am, 1pm) on Saturday, but you do need to make reservations. Tickets are about $15.

**Puerto Vallarta Zoo**

(Camino al Eden 700, Mismaloya | (322) 228-0955 | 10am–6pm daily |
www.zoologicodevallarta.com).
South of PV is the city zoo (*Zoologico de Vallarta*). It's actually in Mismaloya, about 7 miles (12 km) from Downtown and sits in lush forest about 800 meters off the highway.

It's quite simple and small compared to a large city zoo, but it's unique and worth visiting because it's intimate and puts you really close to the animals. It's a great place to go with your young children (or even older animal-loving ones!) and our children, now grown, still enjoy visiting.

There is little more than low fences separating you from the animals, and you can buy a small bag of food to feed them ($5 extra); where else are you encouraged to feed the animals? The jaguars and other predatory cats are more securely fenced off, of course!

The zoo is open all week, and the basic entrance fee is fairly low ($10). But the zoo also sells a special package that lets you interact with tiger, lion, and jaguar cubs ($85).

**Vallarta Botanical Gardens**

(Carretera Barra De Navidad Km. 24, Las Juntas y los Veranos| (322) 223-6182 | 9am–6pm Tue–Sun | www.vbgardens.org). Just 7 miles (12 km) south of the zoo is another option for the nature-lovers—Vallarta Botanical Gardens. It's well in from the coast, so it's a peaceful escape surrounded by a magnificent array of exotic plants.

The gardens are famous for their variety of orchids housed in greenhouses, but there are also about 3,000 species of plant in the 20-acre site. There is a museum in the visitors center (*Hacienda del Oro*), gift shop, and a pleasant little restaurant with views of the grounds down toward a river where you can while away the afternoon. It's a nice place to do some relatively easy walks on groomed trails but not good for anyone mobility impaired. From December through March, it's open 7 days. Entrance costs $10.

View of Los Muertos Beach from the Municipal Pier in Puerto Vallarta.
Photo by Bud Ellison

## What to Do

Puerto Vallarta has no shortage of things for you to do: from taking romantic strolls along exotic white sandy beaches to taking boat or adventure tours, and from exploring centuries-old historic sites to enjoying fine dining and taking in the buzz of PV's nightlife.

But many of these options are designed for the general tourist, and not all of the options you'll see advertised in tourist leaflets are what they seem to be. Being such a popular coastal resort destination, PV does have some excellent restaurants, worthwhile day trips out of the city, and locations that boast genuinely awe-inspiring ocean views. It's just a matter of knowing where to go.

Here are some of the activities we love to do, as well as others you may be interested in and are well worth taking the time to do.

### Romantic Options

Puerto Vallarta is really popular with honeymooning couples and people seeking a romantic getaway, but that's hardly surprising when you consider the weather, the tropical setting, and the Pacific waters with famously striking sunsets.

Many of the guests we've welcomed to *Casa Dos Cisnes* over the years have come here for exactly these reasons, and we've advised them on the best options available in the area. Here are just a few of our favorite things to do; we're still incurable romantics after all of these years!

Sunset over Bandera Bay, Puerto Vallarta. Photo by Terri Bateman

**Walk Along the Malecón** – This is the best way to get a feel for Puerto Vallarta. We like to go in the morning, when the sun is still behind the hillside (usually until 10am or so) and it's sparsely populated, primarily by locals going to work, fisherman, and joggers or walkers. It's nice to see the town when it's just coming to life and the air is still cool with optimism for another beautiful day. After a long walk or jog, we'll grab a coffee at Dee's (see "Dining Out"), and maybe something sweet (cinnamon rolls with frosting!) or at Eric's Paris Café (mentioned previously on page 10 but worth repeating!).

If you're not an early riser, that's not a problem. The Malecón is lovely morning, noon, or night. Take photos with the bronze sculptures that you'll encounter along the way, created by well-known Mexican artists. Sand and rock sculptures also abound. For a local flavor, listen to the concerts held at Plaza de Armas, beneath the shadow of the city's iconic cathedral. Or watch for the "*Voladores*" (fliers) swinging upside-down from high atop a pole, in an ancient ritual from Veracruz.

The location is popular for local families on most nights and the later it gets, the more popular it becomes as the nightclubs come into full swing. So, if you like to dance, visit Mandala or La Vaquita around midnight or later.

**Stroll Los Muertos Beach** – This is the most popular beach in PV and is the easiest beach to access. It's a stone's throw to Zona Romántica where so many of the city's boutiques, restaurants, and bars are. The very southern stretches of the beach are generally more peaceful, making it the perfect escape from the bustle on the streets. The best time for romance is as the sun sets slowly into the Pacific Ocean. Just south of Los Muertos Beach (and closer to *Casa Dos Cisnes*) is something of a hidden gem—Las Amapas Beach. It's more peaceful than its neighbor to the north. In fact, it's a good spot for a picnic. To get there, follow the narrow path that leads behind *El Púlpito* (The Pulpit), a rocky outcrop that marks the end of Los Muertos Beach.

**Arrange Dinner on the Beach** – Two of our favorite restaurants, Vista Grill (known as El Dorado during the day) and La Palapa (see "Dining Out"), have tables directly on the beach, lit by torches and candlelight. Start early and catch the sunset with cocktails, followed by a sumptuous meal to the sound of soft jazz and light waves. This is the definition of "romantic."

**Dinner with a View** – There are multiple restaurant venues with views overlooking the city and/or ocean; three of our favorites are La Iguana, Barcelona Tapas, and La Capella.

**Take a Boat Trip to Yelapa** – Water taxis from Los Muertos Pier will take you south to the town of Yelapa. The journey takes an hour but, on the way, you'll see intimate deserted coves and some of the area's most spectacular coastal homes. Once at Yelapa, hike inland to the local waterfall, head into the forest on horseback, or just relax, do some swimming, and get a light meal at a beachfront restaurant before catching the boat returning to Los Muertos Pier.

## Beaches

PV is famous for its beaches and deserves to be. In the high season, you can expect large crowds to flock to the main ones, but there are quieter, lesser-known beaches worth discovering. If we're going to leave our pool and put our feet in the sand, these are the beaches we go to:

Taking in the Pacific Ocean from Conchas Chinas, Puerto Vallarta.
Photo by Daryl Mitchell

**Los Muertos Beach & Pier** – Los Muertos Beach stretches for a mile (1.6 km) south of Río Cuale and is without doubt the most popular beach in PV. It's never empty, with locals and vacationers flocking there, so it's not the best beach for peace and quiet—either at midday or midnight.

For a day at the beach, we reserve chairs at the El Dorado Beach Club (we arrange a similar service for guests renting our villa). The only downside to this area is the steady stream of hawkers; but just wag your finger, say "no" and take another sip of your margarita. Rinse. Repeat.

The beach is excellent for swimming or just wading into the waves, though not for more vigorous water activities, like surfing. We recommend it for evening and night-time strolls (romantic or otherwise).
Los Muertos Pier is an icon of modern PV, mainly because of its artistic design, with a wide, gently winding walkway and a large metal sail-like sculpture at its end. It's an excellent vantage point for photos of the bay and the beach, and at night, it's lit by a colorful array of lights.

**Conchas Chinas Beach** – This strand is just a short distance from us. Not very many people know about it for some reason, so it's where we like to go for a lazy day if we're leaving the house. When we spend a day here, we like to combine it with a trip to La Playita Restaurant at the Lindo Mar Resort, a little further south. Or better yet, get yourself a chaise lounge right in front of the restaurant and be served margaritas on the beach!

The area has small, intimate rocky coves, making it both one of the most striking beaches and perfect for avoiding the city crowds. It's popular for snorkeling and fishing, but new developments in the area may mean more people discovering this hidden treasure.

Conchas Chinas beach
Photo via: MLS Vallarta

**Playa Mismaloya** – A 30-minute drive south from *Casa Dos Cisnes* is Mismaloya Beach. There has been a lot of development here over the years, but this small strand has calm waters and scenic views, so it's still a good place to relax. You can hire a private *panga* (a small motorboat) to take you to Los Arcos, a protected marine park considered one of the best diving and snorkeling sites in the region. Snorkeling equipment is usually available on the boats and included in the price you negotiate. Always agree on a fixed price BEFORE you step onto the boat.

**Boca de Tomatlán** – Only a few miles further south along the coast is Boca de Tomatlán. It's a small village, so is a complete escape from the commercialism of PV (and even Mismaloya), and with several good, local restaurants, it's an excellent place to explore authentic traditional dishes on the beach. It's also a stop for boats from PV on their way to smaller, more remote beaches like Las Animas, Quimixto and Yelapa. We sometimes hike from Boca to Las Animas Beach, have lunch there and take a boat back.

## Water Activities

Several good beaches offer a range of water activities, including Los Muertos in town (see above). But the beaches further north, in the Zona Hotelera and Marina Vallarta, arguably offer the best options. Hotel resorts as well as independent companies offer jet skis for hire, parasailing, and banana-boat rides daily, especially in high season (December–April). They're usually available on weekends all year round.

If you enjoy water and shoreline activities, here are some of the best options to do:

### Beach Hikes

If you like to hike, there are interesting routes along the beaches and rocky coastline. None are particularly strenuous, and as long as you don't mind tackling some rocky outcrops, the routes can be navigated by everyone.

Our particular favorite has been the hike from Los Muertos Beach to Conchas Chinas Beach. A winding concrete stairway links the end of the Malecón to Calle Santa Barbara, close to the rear of the Puerto Vallarta Beach Club. Walk south along Calle Santa Barbara, which takes you through villa-clad neighborhoods briefly before opening out onto the sand. From there, hike along a series of little beaches, tidal pools, intimate coves, and smoothened rocky outcrops. The entire route should only take an hour or two, but you can stop to swim, snorkel, or sunbathe, so take the whole day if you wish. Just be sure to bring a sun hat, sunscreen, bug repellent (in the summer season when the weather can be humid), and wear light walking shoes. Note that, as of this writing, there is considerable construction along Calle Santa Barbara, making parts of the hike less enjoyable.

As mentioned above, we also like to hike from Boca de Tomatlán to Las Animas Beach, have lunch and take a boat back to Boca. There's a footpath that follows the coastline, much of it through the trees on the hill overlooking the sea, so you won't be in direct sunshine the whole way.

Playa de Mismaloya, south of Puerto Vallarta. Photo by Lucy Nieto

**Sea Life Spotting**

Bay cruises are available throughout the year, which promise an "up-close-and-personal" experience with local marine life. You can catch glimpses of manta rays as they leap from the water, or dolphins, which are often spotted following the boats. During turtle season (late summer through fall), there are tours to turtle nesting beaches where you can watch baby turtles surface through the sand and scuttle down into the sea.

And from late in the year to early in the new year, whale watchers will be delighted as migrating humpback whales breed and spout throughout the bay, sometimes visible with young calves from the beach or pier (see "Whale Watching" below). Occasionally, we see the whales while eating breakfast from our terrace, but generally you have to get in a boat and get further out. It's a hit and miss activity. We've gone years where we went out and saw nothing, but just last year we had a super day when we had several coming up right beside our boat for an extended period of time. It only has to happen once to have a lasting memory; these creatures are big!

For a special treat, rent a boat and cruise the bay, searching for sea life and enjoying the refreshing water with a quick swim or snorkeling break (see below).

**Diving & Snorkeling**

At the southern end of Banderas Bay, just off the coast of Mismaloya, are Los Arcos (The Arches), sea rocks named for the arching grottoes cut into their granite base. The Los Arcos Marine Sanctuary is one of the best snorkeling grounds in PV, with some of the most exotic and colorful fish found amongst the tropical coral. You can take a tour from Marina Vallarta but, for a more private experience, just go down to Mismaloya Beach (described above) and engage one of the local *pangas* (motorboats) to take you there. It will be significantly cheaper and a more authentic experience than going on an "official tour" with 20 "new friends."

Los Arcos, a favorite location to snorkel or scuba dive. Photo: Pinterest

Scuba-diving is also recommended at Los Arcos. Many of the reefs are shallow, so it's perfect for both experienced divers and beginners. Night dives are also possible.

If you need to rent gear, you should consider:

**Chico's Dive Shop** (Paseo Díaz Ordáz 772, Centro | (322) 222-1895 | 10am–5am daily | www.chicos-diveshop.com). From US & Canada 1805-617-0121. Scuba diving costs $98. Snorkeling $40.

**Vallarta Undersea** (Calle Proa, Local 22, Marina Vallarta | (322) 209-0025, (956) 287-3832 | 8am–6pm Mon–Sat | www.vallartaundersea.com.mx). Scuba diving costs $125. Snorkeling $69.

**Whale Watching**

Banderas Bay welcomes large numbers of whales from December through April for mating season. This is the best time to take a whale watching tour from one of the various tour operators in town and see a humpback or even an orca but be aware that seeing a whale is a bit hit-and-miss.

Whales play seasonally in Bandera Bay, Puerto Vallarta. Photo by Terri Bateman

On occasion (especially when good friends or family are visiting), we rent a yacht for a day or a half-day, because even if we don't see a whale, we at least enjoy a pleasant and relaxing day out. It's not cheap; between $1,500 and $4,000 depending on the yacht and crew size we want, which in turn depends on whether we're going out together or have invited guests. If you don't want to spend at that level, or you don't mind being on a boat with other people, there are companies that offer whale watching excursions. Some companies offer a "See or Come Back" deal, so you get another chance if the whales aren't visible the first time you tour. Others have hydrophones on board, so you can hear the whales talking.

**Ecotours** (Ignacio L. Vallarta 243, Col. E. Zapata | (322) 223-3130, (322) 222-6606 | 8am–7pm Mon–Sat, 10am–2pm Sun | www.ecotoursvallarta.com) offer two 3.5-hr tours daily in season (Dec to Mar) $100.

**Sociedad Cooperativa Corral del Risco** (Av. El Anclote 1, Manz. 17, Corral del Risco | (329) 291-6298 | www.puntamitacharters.com). Whale watching and snorkeling around Marietas Islands for up to 10 people ($16/person). Full 2-hr tour $30/person, includes snorkeling in Marietas National Aquatic Park. $90/person gets you access to Playa del Amor.

## Surfing

We're not surfers but we have friends who are. The best time for surfing is between June and December, when waves are high and water temperatures are warm, averaging 80°F (27°C). There is surfing available on the main beaches, like Los Muertos, but experienced surfers won't find the location particularly interesting. If you're a passionate surfer, you'll want to visit the best surf spots, all of which are north of PV. Sayulita and Punta de Mita, both renowned surfing locations, are about an hour from the airport, so quite a distance if you're starting out from Conchas Chinas.

La Lancha is a surfer-only beach around 50 minutes from Downtown PV. It's a lengthy journey, but the beach is long and deserted. Burros Point is close by, has a reputation as the best surfing spot in the region, and is recommended for beginner and intermediate surfers.

Surfing is also popular at Mismaloya and Yelapa. Sited between them is Quimixto Beach. Because it's not accessible by land, it's usually quiet. The best way to get there is by water taxi from Los Muertos Pier (45 mins) or Boca de Tomatlán (20 mins).

The website (www.surfpuertovallarta.info) is the main go-to site for surfers. It provides up-to-date surfing conditions, weather reports, and surf shop links. So, check it before heading out or booking an excursion.

## Fishing

Puerto Vallarta is recognized for its excellent sport fishing, with 500 lb. marlin known to be landed. You'll find a lot of tour companies that specialize in deep sea fishing and offer day charters and tours for anything from four to 12 hours, even overnight. Most are based in Marina Vallarta, with a few more options in Nuevo Vallarta. Rates can range dramatically ($100–$600), depending on the boat size, tour time, and party number.

You can also hire a panga for a full or half-day trip into the bay, and hunt the likes of Spanish mackerel, sea bass, and snapper. This option is perfect from small coastal villages, like Mismaloya and Boca de Tomatlán. Pangas can be $50–$60 per hour.

If you prefer shoreline fishing, the most popular spots are Los Muertos Pier and the southern end of Los Muertos Beach, with mullet, mackerel and snapper often caught. The good news is you don't need a license to fish from the shore (¡Viva México!), only from a boat.

**CharterDreams** (Marina Las Palmas II, Locales 1, Marina Vallarta | (322) 221-0690 | www.charterdreams.com). Fishing trips from $550.

**Puerto Vallarta Fishing** (Terminal Marítima, Los Peines Pier, Marina Vallarta | (322) 222-4935 | www.puertovallartafishing.net). From US & Canada 1-866-217-9704. Fishing trips from $345.

## Land Activities

As well as the obvious beach and water-related activities, PV has lots of land activities. A lot of our guests are golfers, but there are also a variety of more adventurous options, such as horseback riding and tours above the jungle canopy.

### Golf

We rarely golf in PV because our friends here are exponentially better than we are and competitive, too! So, it doesn't lend itself to a relaxing time out for us. But we'll tell you what we know.

There are two golf courses in PV, both near the airport. The Marina Vallarta Golf Club overlooks the bay, while the Vista Vallarta Golf Club sits a few miles east of the airport.

The remaining good golf destinations are in the neighboring state of Nayarit, so quite a distance away. But two that might be worth the trek are the Jack Nicklaus-designed Pacifico Golf Course at the Four Seasons' Punta Mita Golf Club, which boasts stunning ocean views from the Punta Mita peninsula, and the Greg Norman-designed Litibu Golf Club just a few miles further north.

Green fees can range from quite reasonable to quite a lot—in fact, from over $100 to over $250. Taxi drivers are happy to take you to whichever course you like since they're all fairly easy to access. For more information, you might look at GolfAdvisor.com

**Marina Vallarta Golf Club** (Paseo de la Marina | (322) 221-0073 | www.marinavallartagolf.com).
**Vista Vallarta** (Circuito Universidad #653, Col. El Pitillal | (322) 290-0030 | www.clubcorp.com/Clubs/Vista-Vallarta-Club-de-Golf).

**Punta Mita Golf Club** (Ramal Carretera Federal 200 (km 19), Bahia de Banderas, Nayarit | (329) 291-5590 | www.fourseasons.com).

**Litibu Golf Club** (Carr. Punto de Mita, Litibu, Higuera Blanca, 63734 Nayarit | (329) 298-4091 | www.rivieranayarit.com/activities/golf/litibu).

**Horseback Riding**

Almost all of the horseback riding activities commence at family ranches in towns in the foothills of the Sierra Madre mountain chain, like Las Palmas. Unfortunately, beaches around the PV area don't allow horses, so horseback riding is confined to the smaller coastal villages and towns, like Bucerias, Sayulita, and San Francisco (San Pancho).

There are riding adventure tours available, which bring you into the jungle areas. These are perfect options for a day trip. You can also take longer rides; from eight hours to overnight. One of the most popular goes into the Sierra Madre. Although it's normal for lunch to be included in your tour fee, always remember to bring plenty of water with you. The sun here can be intense.

**Rancho Mi Chaparrita** (Manuel Rodriguez Sanchez 14, Riviera Nayarit, Sayulita | (329) 291-3112/298-2559 | www.michaparrita.com). Prices at $50 (1hr 20m), $90 (2hrs 20m).

**Puerto Vallarta Tours** (Manuel M Dieguez 404, Alta Vista | (322) 222-4935 | 9am–2:30pm Mon–Fri | www.puertovallartatours.net). Prices from $63. Call toll-free from US & Canada 1-866-217-9704, or PV 1-800-007-8386.

### Canopy Tours

Several canopy tour operators have offices in Downtown PV, offering zip-lining at a range of different locations. The best are set in the Los Veranos Ecological Preserve, along the Mismaloya River (south) and in Sayulita (the latter being an hour north, so we've never been there, but have heard about it). Most provide a lot more than just zipping down cables at 35 mph, with horseback riding, swimming, canoeing, forest trekking, and sometimes beach activities on offer. It's easy to arrange a full day of activities.

Be aware that there are often age and weight restrictions for certain activities (usually 250 pounds maximum). And remember to consider the weather, especially during the rainy season when there's a regular threat of thunder storms in the afternoons.

Zip-lining: a thrilling adventure in the jungle hillsides of Puerto Vallarta Photo: Vallarta Adventures

We recommend these canopy tour companies because of their excellent safety record:

**Los Veranos Canopy Tours** (Francisca Rodríguez 336, Emiliano Zapata | (322) 223-0504/0649 | 8am–6pm Mon–Sat; 9am–5pm Sun | www.canopytours-vallarta.com). Prices from $89 (web). Call toll-free from US & Canada 1-800-396-9168.

**Puerto Vallarta Tours** (Manuel M Dieguez 404, Alta Vista | (322) 222-4935 | 9am–2:30pm Mon–Fri | www.puertovallartatours.net). Prices from $63. Call toll-free from US & Canada 1-866-217-9704, or PV 1-800-007-8386.

**Rancho Mi Chaparrita** (Manuel Rodriguez Sanchez 14, Riviera Nayarit, Sayulita | (329) 291-3112/298-2559 | www.michaparrita.com). Prices from $85.

**ATV/Dune Buggy Tours**

We haven't been on an ATV tour for a while, but it's an excellent way to experience the rustic charm of the rural communities in the hills around the city. Some tours take you along the coast and others on jungle courses along the riverbanks north, south, and east of the city.

Tours are available year-round, run for three or four hours with packages costing between $70 and $160 (combos with zip-lining cost $300–$400). Keep in mind the rainy season (July–

October) is hot and wet, while courses are quite dusty the rest of the year. You'll also need to have a valid driver's license.

**Unique ATV Tours** (Río de La Plata 248, López Mateos | (322) 223-3516 | 9am–5pm daily | www.uniqueatvtours.com). Prices from $67. Call from US (602) 283-2547; toll-free 1-866-391-6109.

**Estigo ATV Tours** (Honduras 135, 5 de Diciembre | (322) 223-8143 | 9am–7pm Mon–Fri; 9am–2pm Sat | www.estigoscooters.com) Prices from $93. Call toll-free from US 1-801-923-2019, or Canada 1-864-800-0776.

**Exercise**

If you're a jogger, avoid the cobblestone streets and head to the *Malecon* in the early mornings while it's still fresh outside and the sun hasn't risen over the hills; you won't be alone unless you're a really early riser, but you'll be able to run for a fairly long stretch while observing the vendors just setting up their stalls and the fishermen bringing in their catch. For yoga enthusiasts, there are several studios in PV (www.yogafinder.com) or hire an instructor to come to your villa (our concierge or manager arranges this for our guests). And for those who really want to shake things up, visit Plaza Lazaro Cardenas in the Romantic Zone where Zumba classes (open to the public) will wake you up bright and early at 8:00 a.m. most mornings. There are also fitness clubs in PV which offer day passes; although we haven't visited one personally, friends of ours go to The Fit Club at Rivera Molino Local 9, Ignacio L. Vallarta 130, Centro. Or, if you're lucky, your villa comes with a gym (like ours!), so you don't need to leave home to stay fit.

**Spas**

Multiple day spas are available in town (Tripadvisor is a good source) or in the larger hotels to the north (e.g. the "Ohtli" at the Marriott or the "Spa" at the Westin), or, if you've rented a villa with a concierge service or manager (like ours!), spa service providers should be able to come to your villa and provide manicures, pedicures, and our favorite: couples' massages.

**Day Trips**

When we're in Puerto Vallarta, we pretty much stay in Puerto Vallarta. That's mainly because we are just happy that, for once, we're not traveling or that we've gotten away from the winter in Europe.

But if you're tired of town and want to get away for just the day, there are a number of interesting trips you can make. None of these fall into any kind of "must see" category, but each one is interesting and provides insight into the natural beauty, the history, and the simplicity of Mexico. Your form of transportation will, in part, determine your destination but here are a few options we think you'll enjoy.

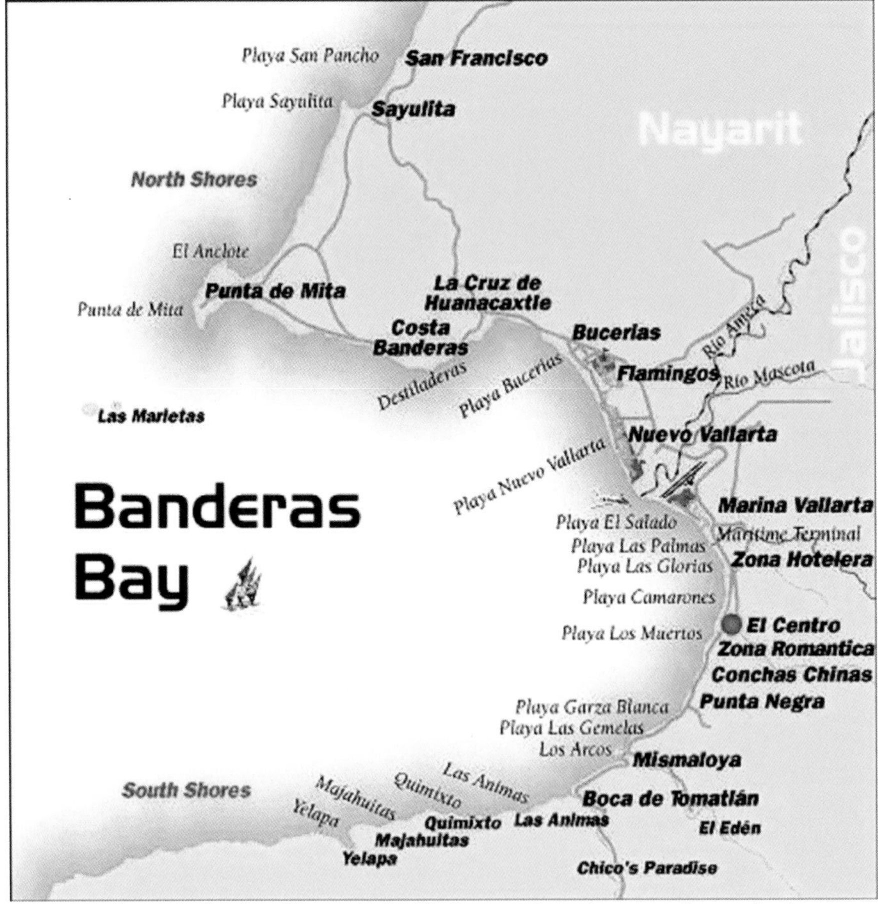


Puerto Vallarta hugs Banderas Bay, on the Pacific Ocean, and stretches across the state line between Jalisco and Nayarit. There are many day trips worth taking outside Puerto Vallarta, from Yelapa in the south to San Francisco in the north.

**San Sebastián del Oeste**

It's a long journey from PV to this small mountain town (a couple of hours depending on where you're starting from... and who's driving :)), but it's peaceful and quaint, a step back in time. You can visit one of the beautiful historic haciendas or take in a tour of a local coffee plantation or gold mine. There are several good restaurants worth whiling away a lazy afternoon in; our favorite is Montebello Restaurante (www.facebook.com/Montebello-Restaurante-San-Sebastián-del-Oeste-167992023360992/).

There are day tour operators if you don't want to drive (www.superiortoursvallarta.com goes to places like San Sebastián, San Pancho, Sayulita and Riviera Nayarit), and if you do drive, there are simple, inexpensive accommodations in and near town at which you can stay overnight.

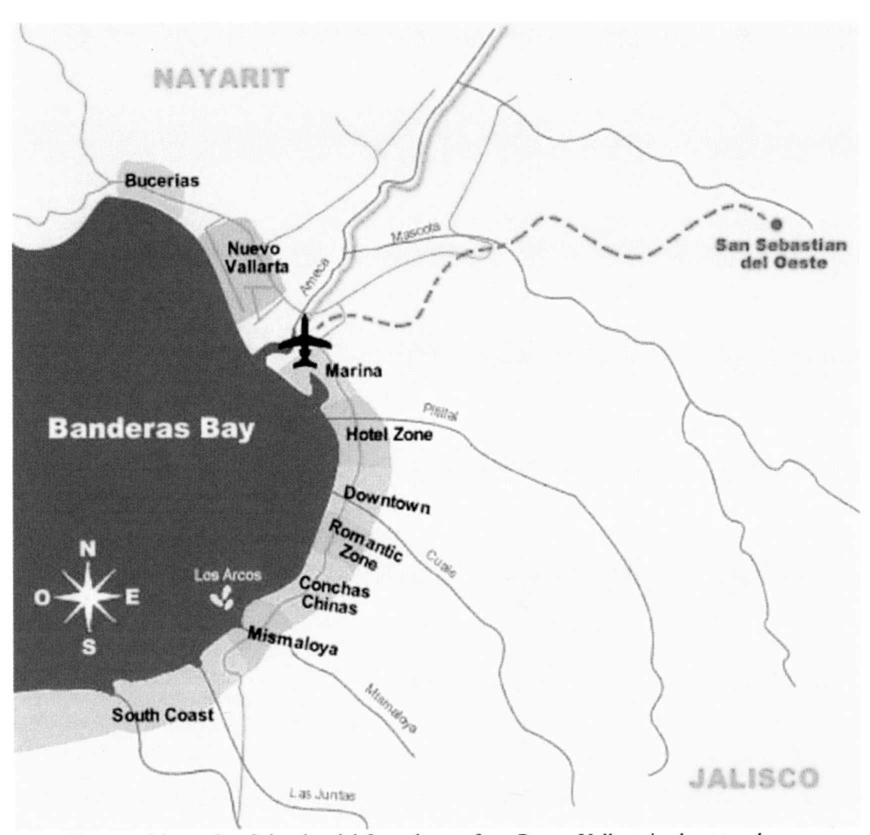


You can drive to San Sebastian del Oeste by car from Puerto Vallarta in about two hours.

**Las Galeritas** (Camino a La Galerita 62, San Sebastián del Oeste | (322) 297-3040 | www.lagalerita.com.mx/en). About $120/night including breakfast.

**Hotel Mansion Real** (5 de Mayo No. 36 A, Centro, San Sebastian del Oeste | (55) 6413-8008 | mansion-real.jalisco-hotels.com/en). About $100/night.

**Hotel del Puente** (Calle Lerdo de Tejada 3, San Sebastian del Oeste | (322) 297-2834). About $40/night. Actually, this is where we've stayed, and it's clean Mexican simplicity. You don't need to spend more.

**Sayulita**

PV's northern neighbor, Sayulita, is a lively beach town about an hour north, known for its laid-back, almost hippie vibe. It's popular for its pristine beach, excellent surfing, dining, and shopping, but there are also zip-lining and horseback riding tours in the area. In fact, it's pretty much impossible to get bored in Sayulita. If you don't fancy the lengthy drive, there is a regular bus service from PV every 20 minutes between 6am and 10pm. The journey takes about 90 mins, and tickets cost around $2. Be forewarned, however, the buses are very basic and are not comfortable by most people's standards for this long of a journey.

Sayulita, known for its casual vibe and outstanding surfing Photo: Huffington Post

**San Francisco** (San Pancho)

Just five minutes further north of Sayulita is San Francisco (also known as San Pancho). It's quieter than its nearest neighbor, and in many ways prettier. It's surrounded by palm groves and virgin jungle, a sandy beach to stroll along backed by a tranquil lagoon, and beachfront cafés to spend an afternoon in. The main street has several fine restaurants and bars. There is also a local golf club, and (in season) polo matches with world-class players in action.

**Yelapa**

Set on the southern reaches of Banderas Bay, Yelapa isn't easy to access, but worth making the effort. You can only get there by boat either from Los Muertos Pier in PV (45 mins) or Boca de Tomatlán (after Mismaloya, 20 mins). The beach town is popular among surfers and fishing enthusiasts, but there is also hang gliding, hiking, or good old-fashioned beach and café lounging too.

**Marietas Islands**

A group of small islands off the coast from Punta Mita, these are one of the most stunning places in the region. They're protected and recognized for their bio-diversity and natural beauty, but they are also a magnet for snorkeling, scuba diving, and paddle surfing.

Love Beach in the Marieta Islands National Park, off the Puerto Vallarta coast.
Photo: Jose Paul Sharvin

Playa del Amor (also known as the "Hidden Beach"), only accessible by swimming 75m (200 feet) from your boat, is a "must see." But the number of visitors per day is very limited and access must be reserved a few days in advance. You get a wristband for $90–$150. The only way to these islands is by boat, but it's only a 20-minute trip from Punta de Mita.

In winter, a trip to the islands will most likely involve a glimpse of humpback whales. Playa del Amor is closed Monday and Tuesdays.

> **Sociedad Cooperativa Corral del Risco** (Av. El Anclote 1, Manz. 17, Corral del Risco | (329) 291-6298 | www.puntamitacharters.com). Whale watching and snorkeling around Marietas Islands for up to 10 people ($16/person). Full 2-hr tour $30/person, includes snorkeling in Marietas National Aquatic Park. $90/person gets you access to Playa del Amor.
>
> **Vallarta Adventures** (Calle Mástil 13, Marina Vallarta | (322) 226-8413 | 8am–2pm; 4.30pm–7pm Mon–Sat | www.vallarta-adventures.com). Full 4.5-hr tour from $149/person with access to Playa del Amor. Call from US & Canada 1-888-526-2238.

**Dining Out**

As we've already mentioned, we mostly dine in. That's because at *Casa Dos Cisnes* we've got the best views of the ocean in Puerto Vallarta, a gourmet chef who lives in the house, and dinner that starts whenever we come downstairs.

To be honest, there are great restaurants in PV and that contributed quite a lot to our choice of city in which to build a home. We generally go out for dinner once or twice a week, and a few times for lunch just to have a change of scenery and give the staff some time off.

Dining out in Puerto Vallarta tends to be a casual affair—even at the best restaurants, many people are in dressy shorts (probably tourists) or slacks/jeans. Nowhere we know of requires a jacket. For the finer restaurants, we would say smart casual for men, and resort wear for women. For the more casual restaurants, almost anything goes!

Although there are hundreds of restaurants to choose from, we generally frequent the ones that have lasted the test of time. Many restaurants here don't survive their first year, but those that have been around for a while are well-run, offer great food in nice atmospheres with prices that correspond to value for quality. Here are some of our favorites, with a price key so you know what to pay:

***Price Key** – **$** ($15); **$$** ($16–$30); **$$$** ($31–$45); **$$$$** ($46–$60); **$$$$$** ($60+)*

### Seafood

**La Palapa** (Púlpito 105-3, Emiliano Zapata | (322) 222-5225 | 8:30am–11:30pm daily | www.lapalapapv.com | $–$$$).
Right on Los Muertos beachfront, it's an excellent choice for beach dining, especially for breakfast and in the evening watching the sunset. The restaurant was one of the first in PV, and is still operated by the original owners, the Perez family. The menu includes international dishes with modern twists and imaginative seafood, and between food quality, location, and the soft Latin jazz atmosphere, the price is justified. Daytime sees hawkers in action, but just wave them off and continue your meal.

**El Dorado/Vista Grill** (Calle Pulpito 102, Amapas | (322) 223-5568 | 11am–5pm daily | www.eldoradopvr.com | $–$$).
Now owned by the Perez family, who also operate La Palapa across the street, this open-air restaurant on Los Muertos Beach is reminiscent of 1960's Puerto Vallarta, but with an updated ambience and menu. Noted as a romantic place to dine on the beach, it operates under two names, El Dorado Beach Club during the day and Vista Grill in the evenings. Prior to owning a home here, this was our first-night go-to restaurant, to get us into a tropical mood.

**Pez Limon** (Las Rosas 278, Villa Las Flores | (322) 688-1865 | 12pm–7pm daily | $–$$).
A new addition to PV's hip dining scene, Pez Limon is the creation of the chef/owner Joel Ornelas of Tintoque (see

"Gourmet" below). Don't be concerned as you approach on a dirt road in a "barrio," nor that it's set in a large warehouse very near the airport; upon arrival, you'll quickly realize this isn't your average taco restaurant. This is "local Mexico" and the cuisine focuses on traditional Mexican tacos, tostadas, and soups, but with new twists of flavors. And while the restaurant has no views, its inventive menu and vibrant atmosphere more than make up for it. Note: this is only for lunch, albeit the Mexico lunch hour runs quite late.

**Ocho Tostadas** (Quilla esquina Proa Local 28-29, Marina Vallarta | (322) 209-1508 | 11am–6pm daily | www.facebook.com/OchoTostadas | $–$$).
Ocho Tostadas has several locations in town, including on the restaurant "strip-mall" at the entrance to Fluvial Vallarta, behind the Agustin Flores Contreras Stadium (*Estadio Municipal Agustin Flores Contreras*) across from the Sheraton Hotel (known as Freddy's, and this one at the Marina. It's a popular, casual seafood destination, but has some of the best shrimp cocktails, ceviche, and shrimp empanadas anywhere in PV. It's inexpensive with a no frills décor (although the new Fluvial location is more upscale and modern). We think of Ocho Tostadas as a great lunch choice whenever we're on the north side of town. Mostly locals eat here, which means it's good!

**El Barracuda** (Paraguay 1290, 5 de Diciembre | (322) 222-4034 | 1pm–10pm Mon & Tue; 12pm–12am Wed–Sun | www.elbarracuda.com | $).
This open beach shack serves an excellent seafood lunch with superb views of Banderas Bay with a funky interior. Its specialties include grilled shrimp tacos, tuna sashimi, and mariscos dinamita (shrimp, octopus, and fish rice dish). An added attraction is the turtle beach close by where diners can see turtles lay eggs (in season) and even catch a glimpse of whales thrashing in the bay in winter. We go here a lot for lunch. Note: Cash only is accepted.

Barracuda Restaurant: the best beachfront restaurant for fresh fish tacos, ocean breezes, and casual dining day or night Photo: Pinterest

**Joe Jack's Fish Shack** (Basilio Badillo 212, Emiliano Zapata | (322) 222-2099 | 12pm–11pm daily | www.joejacks-fishshack.com | $)
Another casual spot for lunch or dinner, Joe Jack's has been around for over 10 years, serving reasonably priced drinks and meals in the popular Zona Romántica. Although lacking in views, the best tables are on the upper floor, where plants and candlelight add atmosphere and ocean breezes still manage to cool the nights.

**Spanish**

**Barcelona Tapas** (Calle Matamoros 906, Centro | (322) 222-0510 | 12pm–12am daily | www.barcelonatapas.net/index-eng.html | $–$$$$).
Perched on top of a building high on a hill, just four blocks from the northern end of the Malecón, Barcelona Tapas offers some of the most beautiful views of the bay and town, day and night (note that you'll climb a substantial amount of stairs for this reward; no elevator!). The menu is Spanish tapas, with both

traditional and seafood paella. If you're indecisive, ask for the chef's specially selected tasting menu, which has six courses including soup, salad, hot and cold tapas, and dessert. It's air-conditioned in the summer, but the windows are removed the rest of the year. Reservations are essential.

## Fine Dining

**Café des Artistes** (Guadalupe Sánchez 740, Centro | (322) 222-3228/3229 | 6pm–11:30pm daily | www.cafedesartistes.com | $$$–$$$$$).
Located three blocks from the northern end of the Malecón (just follow Leona Vicario), Café des Artistes is arguably PV's finest restaurant and was one of the first truly gourmet restaurants established when Puerto Vallarta was "coming of age" in the 80s. It consistently delivers. It has a romantic ambience (a French-Mexican fusion), with candlelit tables, some in a garden courtyard; but it's the gourmet cuisine that makes it truly remarkable. We'd recommend you make a reservation, especially during high season.

Café Des Artistes: Puerto Vallarta's premier dining destination
Photo: Vallarta Lifestyles

**Trio** (Calle Guerrero 264, Centro | (322) 222-2196 | 6pm–11:30pm daily | www.triopv.com/en | $–$$).
Convivial and homey, Trio is another one of PV's first gourmet restaurants that has stood the test of time. This was actually the first gourmet restaurant we went to on one of our first trips here and it continues to delight all these years later. Its menu is mostly Mediterranean, including popular favorites like rack of lamb with fresh mint. We particularly like the huachinango (red snapper) with tequila garlic sauce. Servers are professional, unpretentious, and helpful, but the main reason for its popularity is its consistently fabulous food. The kitchen often stays open until nearly midnight, an added bonus if you like late night dining (or if you're like us and you just can't get your act together on time!).

**The Iguana**
(Calle Zaragoza 445, Centro | (322) 222-1336/1877-218-3248 | 6pm–11pm daily; Sun brunch 9am–2pm | www.casakimberly.com/the-iguana-restaurant-tequila-bar/| $$–$$$).
An enchanting restaurant in Casa Kimberly, the former residence of Richard Burton and Elizabeth Taylor. Saved from ruin by the owner of the Hacienda San Angel Hotel (see below), it has recently been restored to more than its original elegance. The ambience is dramatic with a sweeping staircase topped by a gorgeous painting of Ms. Taylor. One can't help think that the couple that put PV on the tourist map would have approved. The food is excellent, although not Michelin star quality, but it's worth going for the history and stunning decor. You'll see photos of Elizabeth and Richard in PV on the back wall.

**La Capella** (Calle Miramar 363B, Centro | (322) 222-0185 | 5pm–11pm daily; Sun brunch 9am–2pm | www.haciendasanangel.com/cappella | $$–$$$).
A sister restaurant to The Iguana and Hacienda San Angel (below), this relatively new Italian restaurant offers the best and most romantic view of the town's landmark, Our Lady of Guadalupe Church. It has a Colonial Mexican ambience (crystal chandeliers, antique saint statues) and a menu that is solidly Italian, including pizzas, if that's what you want. It's high quality, although not particularly imaginative, but the pastas are

homemade and excellent. We only go here for the views and the ambience. The owner, Janice Chatterton, is the only person in PV to capture Colonial-period Mexican interiors perfectly, and she doesn't miss a detail or spare a centavo in order to do so.

**Hacienda San Ángel Gourmet** (Calle Miramar 336, Centro | (322) 222-2692/221-2277 | 6pm–10pm daily | www.haciendasanangel.com/gourmet | $$–$$$$).
The luxurious hacienda-inspired restaurant of the Hacienda San Ángel boutique hotel offers stunning views of the town and Banderas Bay from its second-floor terrace—not to mention the iconic crown-topped bell-tower of Our Lady of Guadalupe. The Colonial period interiors that the owner, Janice Chatterton, has designed are stunningly done and worth seeing alone. The food is uncomplicated but flavorful. We recommend the red snapper with polenta, or beef served on a bed of mashed potatoes and sautéed spinach. Be sure to make a reservation as the restaurant gives preference to guests staying at the hotel and can be booked full.

**River Café** (Isla Río Cuale, Local 4, Centro | (322) 223-0788/223-0788 | 8am–11pm daily | www.rivercafe.com.mx | $$–$$$).
This riverside restaurant boasts a multilevel terrace set amongst tropical palms beneath the Avenida Vallarta Bridge. It's best to go in summer, when the river level and warm air make the setting pretty and romantic. In the winter, the river is dry, ruining the view, and the air can feel somewhat cold. We recommend it for breakfast (from 8am) and for the evening ambience. It offers international dishes like seafood fettuccine, vegetarian crepes, fried calamari with aioli sauce. You can also enjoy live jazz in the bar Friday and Saturday evenings, with no obligation to dine.

**Tintoque** (Plaza Neptuno, Francisco Medina Ascencio, Marina Vallarta | (322) 221-1460 | 5pm–11pm Sun–Thur; 5pm–12am Fri & Sat | www.tintoque.mx | $$–$$$).
Although located in an unpicturesque "strip-mall" (the up-market Plaza Neptuno at the entrance of Marina Vallarta), Tintoque is an upscale, haute cuisine Mexican restaurant led by renowned local chef, Joel Ornelas (only 30 at the time of

writing!). He trained in Europe and has earned a reputation for reinventing traditional dishes into contemporary creations. The décor matches that trend, styled like a traditional airy hacienda with modern tones. The menu changes almost daily, but everything is made with local seasonal ingredients. We wouldn't normally drive this far from Conchas Chinas to go to a restaurant, but for this one we do. It's that good. Remember, make a reservation before journeying out there.

**Bistro Teresa** (Zarogoza 160 Colonia Centro, Malecón, Centro | (322) 113-0281 | 4:30pm–11:30pm daily | www.facebook.com/bistroteresa | $$–$$$).
Located on the second floor of a corner building directly across from Los Arcos Amphitheater on the Malecón, this contemporary restaurant offers stunning views of the ocean and cathedral, while serving delicious continental cuisine. The restaurant is open air when the weather allows and enclosed in the rainy season or due to the noise from performers across the street. The restaurant is highly recommended for its food as well as attentive and warm service, but the street performer noise from the Malecón has, on occasion, dampened our enthusiasm for dining here.

**Casual Eating**

**La Playita** (Carretera a Barra de Navidad, Km 2.5, Conchas Chinas | (322) 221-5556 | 8am–10pm daily | www.lindomarresort.com | $–$$).
This restaurant, associated with the Lindo Mar Resort, is located a couple of minutes from our villa. It offers inexpensive traditional Mexican dining in an easy-going atmosphere. Breakfast and an expansive weekend brunch buffet (8am–1pm) offer crepes, frittatas, and omelets, while lunch and dinner choices include crispy crab tacos, grilled burgers, and shrimp enchiladas—all in the open ocean air with wonderful views of waves crashing on Conchas Chinas Beach. It's a lovely dining experience, with Mexican simplicity, and seems to be, somehow, a well-kept secret (we almost hate to spill the beans here instead of keeping it for ourselves!). The staff, who have been here since before we started coming to Puerto Vallarta, are as friendly as can be, and always have a table for you.

**La Madalena** (Avenida Francisco Medina Ascencio 2025, Las Glorias | (322) 135-9982 | 1pm–2am daily | www.la-madalena-vallarta.negocio.site/ | $$–$$$).
A trendy restaurant that is designed for sports fans as much as food lovers, La Madalena boasts a delicious menu along with the largest TV screen probably anywhere in PV. The menu is international but with a Mexican tone, with shrimp tacos on jicama taco shells, alongside steak with sautéed mushrooms. Cocktail mixology is a key feature here with a gin cart they will roll out to your table to make whatever martini you desire. Glass exterior walls ensure the restaurant is flooded with light through the day, and there's a terrace if you prefer to eat outdoors.

**La Vaca Argentina** (Francisco Medina Ascencio 2468, Col. Fluvial Vallarta | (322) 224-0908 | 1:30pm–11pm daily | www.lavaca-argentina.com | $$$–$$$$$).
Because PV is on the ocean and in Mexico, its restaurants tend to feature either seafood or Mexican specialties. If it's good beef that you crave, then we'd recommend venturing out to Fluvial to La Vaca Argentina. It's a major steakhouse chain but is famous for its excellent steak and roast dishes. There is indoor and outside seating, although outdoor can be a little noisy given its location on a busy corner facing the main road to the airport. The décor is contemporary, while the big screens are a plus if you want to catch a big game. They used to be in Zona Romántica, which is how we know them.

See also: **El Barracuda**, **Ocho Tostada**, **Pez Limon**, and **Joe Jack's Fish Shack** in **"Seafood"** above.

**For Coffee**

**Dee's Coffee Company** (Francisca Rodríguez 111, Int. 117, Emiliano Zapata, Zona Romántica | (322) 222-1197 | 7am–9pm daily | $).
Dee's serves excellent coffee (especially the espresso!) and a range of sweet snacks, like pastries, pies, cakes, cookies, and cinnamon rolls. You can also get freshly-made sandwiches and frappes, and there is a range of refreshing juices served all day. With its location just a stone's throw from Los Muertos Pier,

it's in the heart of Zona Romantica and perfect for a post-beach walk break.

**For Breakfast**

On Sunday mornings, when our staff is off (although guests who rent the villa benefit from 7-day service), the ONLY place we go is **La Palapa** (see "Seafood" above), a favorite destination for all meals. It's on the beach, relaxing, and serves a first-rate breakfast. You really can't improve on it. The price is a bargain compared to any US or European city, especially when you consider the quality of the food and ambience; the perfect place to start or end the week.

The following restaurants are at about the same price point as La Palapa and also come recommended, although they don't offer the same beautiful beach environment:

**Fredy's Tucán** (Basilio Badillo 245, Emiliano Zapata, Zona Romántica | (322) 223-0778 | 8am–3pm daily | fredystucan.com | $).
If you want a more in-town experience, Fredy's is a favorite of locals and tourists alike, frequently voted "Best Breakfast in Puerto Vallarta." Sitting next door to Hotel Posada de Roger, they serve lunch and dinner as well, and have a full bar, but breakfast is most popular. In fact, it's served until 12:30 every day. Be aware, there's always a big line outside on weekends and sometimes on weekdays, too.

**Coco's Kitchen** (Púlpito 122, Emiliano Zapata, Zona Romantica | (322) 223 0373 | 8am–3:30pm daily; dinner 5pm–10pm Mon–Sat | www.cocoskitchenpv.net | $).
Set in a secluded, tropical plant-filled courtyard, Coco's Kitchen offers friendly service with a nice variety of freshly prepared breakfast items, including special French toast and omelets. The restaurant also offers lunch daily and opens for dinner (although dinner may only be in high season).

**The Pancake House** (Basilio Badillo 289, Emiliano Zapata, Zona Romántica | (322) 222-6272 | 8am–2pm daily | $).

Great for kids and adults alike, The Pancake House offers a great variety of breakfast favorites including (of course) pancakes. But it also serves tasty alternatives like eggs benedict, omelets, and French toast. Prices are low but the service is attentive and efficient. You may have to wait at times, but this generally is due to the restaurant's popularity, especially on the weekends.

## Night Life

We don't go out much at night, being in Puerto Vallarta primarily to work and relax. But if you love the nightlife, here are some places either we've gone to on occasion, or we know our friends go to:

**Jazz Foundation** (Calle Allende 116, Centro | (322) 113-0295 | 5pm–1am daily | www.facebook.com/thejazzfoundation).
Sitting near the northern end of the Malecón, this music venue has an interior more resembling an unfinished warehouse than a jazz club, but the quality of its music makes it one of the most popular in PV. Upstairs you'll find regular live music, jam sessions and other jazz-focused events (entrance fees may vary, around $2–$10), and their restaurant serves good food ($$) to strengthen your resolve for the night ahead. But its great ocean views help make the whole experience unforgettable.

**La Bodeguita del Medio** (Paseo Díaz Ordaz 858, Centro | (322) 223-1585 | 11am–2am daily | www.facebook.com/labodeguitadelmediomx).
Down the street from The Jazz Foundation is a decidedly Latin bar and live music venue. Expect to see salsa and mojitos served up all night, and dancing on a small, intimate dance floor. Live acts do bring some variation, but the friendly atmosphere is constant. No cover charge.
**P'yote Lounge** (Calle Guadalupe Sánchez 716, Centro | (322) 222-3228 | 6pm–11pm daily | www.cafedesartistes.com).
With its Huichol-inspired interior décor, the bar at Café des Artistes has an unmistakably Mexican feel. Thus, it makes sense that P'yote Lounge is famous for its Mexican tapas and

mezcalinis (using mescal, the agave-sourced spirit native to Mexico). It has a bright and relaxed atmosphere, with a piano bar to entertain you.

**Act II Entertainment Stages** (Basilio Badillo 330, Altos, Emiliano Zapata, Zona Romántica | (322) 222-1512 | BO: 4pm |
www.actiientertainment.com).
A multi-genre theater, Act II is a unique events venue in PV. In fact, it's PV's answer to Broadway, hosting touring singers, dancers, comedians, and magicians as well as productions of Mexican and globally recognized musicals and plays. Cabaret is very popular, and there is also the Encore Piano & Wine Bar, an intimate bar where you can round off the night.

**Garbo** (Púlpito 142, Emiliano Zapata, Zona Romántica | (322) 223-5753 | 6pm–2am daily).
Located a little closer to us than the other options we've mentioned, Garbo is a small but intimate venue offering jazz sounds and martinis. As the name suggests, the theme of the bar harps back to more glamorous times, and several of the cocktails on offer reflect that—try the Bette Davis! The jazz singing can be very good, and don't be surprised if the crowd joins in.

Magical Puerto Vallarta in the evening. Photo: Costa Sur

## The Malecón

The Malecón is the heart of PV's nightlife activity, whether you are interested in something casual and low key, or you are set for a more lively night out. There is a variety of all-night dancing venues along Paseo Díaz Ordaz, and the adjoining streets. With some venues, you may need to pre-book tickets on weekends and for special events. If you do, prices can be between $60 and $80, but usually entitle you to an open bar for three to four hours.

This is not our kind of night out, but here are a few nightclubs we know are popular that may interest you.

**Bar Morelos** (Morelos 589, Centro | (322) 237-4524 | 7pm–6am daily | www.facebook.com/BarMorelosPuertoVallart) is sited just off the Malecón, with live music (salsa, Latin, jazz). Fun and lively with tastefully designed surrounds and luxury leather couches.

**Mandala Nightclub** (Paseo Díaz Ordaz 633, Centro | Tickets: (322) 223-0966 | 10pm–6am daily | www.facebook.com/mandalavallarta) is popular with young partiers. High octane atmosphere, pulsating music, and all-night dancing make it perfect if that's your scene.

**La Vaquita** (Paseo Díaz Ordaz 610, Centro | Tickets: (322) 149-1836 | 10pm–6am daily | www.facebook.com/LaVaquitaPuertoVallarta) is another all-night dance venue, and a big hit with Spring Breakers. Stands on the Malecón, and a good option if that appeals to you.

## Shopping

We don't come to Puerto Vallarta for shopping but, inevitably, we've found a few places that have things we don't find easily anywhere else in the world. Over the years, we have bought things here for their originality and value. If you have limited time for shopping, we'd recommend Basilio Badillo which has become PV's hub for boutiques.

You'll find clothing, jewelry, pottery, and even Cuban cigars along this street and others close by.

For more browsing, head to the Río Cuale marketplace where you'll find souvenirs as well as jewelry, clothing, and art; note that bargaining is expected at the marketplace, prices start quite high, and quality can vary significantly.

JEWELRY

**Cassandra Shaw Jewelry** (Calle Basilio Badillo 276, Emiliano Zapata, Zona Romántica | (322) 223-9734 | 9am–9pm Mon–Sat; 10am–6pm Sun | www.cassandrashaw.com). Celebrated for its uniquely crafted sterling silver items with a variety of gemstones, you'll find chunky rings, bracelets and necklaces, as well as more delicate creations.

LEATHERWEAR

**Rolling Stone** (Paseo Diaz Ordaz 802, Centro | (322) 223-1769 | 10am–10pm daily). This is the perfect venue if you're looking for custom-made footwear, but a particular favorite of ours are Rolling Stone's purses. Check out the historic pictures and artifacts from historic Puerto Vallarta upstairs, where on-sale items are also located.

CLOTHING

**Luisa's** (Juárez 144, Centro | (322) 222-5042 | 10am–7pm Mon–Sat). For both resort wear and traditional women's clothes, head to Luisa's owned and run by one of the city's most highly regarded dressmakers.

**Maracuya**, next door to the El Dorado on Pulpito. This relatively new shop carries lovely handmade bags from Oaxaca, linen clothing, locally made jewelry, art, etc.

**Suceso at Hildago 113** – If you're looking for something unique, this store features hand-painted, one of a kind blouses and dresses. They are now represented at a store on Michigan Avenue in Chicago.

BEACHWEAR

**Zingara** (Paseo Diaz Ordaz 822, Int. A, Centro | (322) 222-3509 | 11am–10pm Mon–Fri; 11am–11pm Sat & Sun | www.zingarastore.com).

If you need a new bathing suit, go to the Malecón right near Rolling Stone. The store offers a nice selection of separately sold bathing suits and cover-ups.

HOME DECOR

**Banderas Bay Trading Company** (Constitución 319, Int. A, Emiliano Zapata | (322) 223-4352 | 10am–6pm Mon–Fri; 10am–4pm Sat | www.banderasbaytradingcompany.com).

When building our Colonial-Mexican style home, it was difficult to find home décor that blended traditional Colonial design with the beach vibes of Puerto Vallarta. In fact, we bought most decorations in Guadalajara, Tlaquepaque, and Tonala. But we did discover Peter Bowman's Banderas Bay Trading Company, which has a nice selection of Colonial period design with a twist. We've found beautiful candleholders, pottery, stonework, and furniture to perfectly accent the style and feel of our home.

GLASS

**Mundo de Cristal** (Av. Insurgentes 333, Emiliano Zapata, Zona Romantica | (322) 222-4157 | 9am–7pm Mon–Fri; 9am–2pm Sat | mundodecristal.com.mx/eng/).

Most of the glassware in our house comes from Mundo de Cristal. It is classic Mexican fare, and unmistakable.

HUICHOL ART

**Galería La Indígena** (Juárez 628, El Centro | (322) 223-0800 | 10am–8pm Mon–Fri; 10am–6pm Sat).

If you're looking for Mexican hand crafts and art, the best places to go by far are Guadalajara and Mexico City. But we have bought some interesting pieces of ceramics Downtown at Galería La Indígena. You'll pay considerably more than you would in the towns noted above, but the quality is good.

GALLERIES

There are a number of art galleries that have a name in their own right. Almost none of the art leans toward our taste, with the exception of Evelyne Boren's. We have a watercolor of hers purchased in 1986 at PV airport; as you can imagine, the airport was much smaller with almost no shops or restaurants at the time. The art was merely hung on the walls and in many cases sold by the artists themselves! PV is still a relatively small city, yet for its size, it has an amazing number of galleries.

One of the best ways to view the city's galleries is to participate in its "Art Walk" which takes place Wednesday evenings from 6pm–10pm from late October to late May. You'll get to visit several galleries on the route, exhibiting paintings, sculptures, ceramics, and jewelry by some of the most highly regarded national and international artists. For more information and a map, visit the Art Walk website at http://www.puertovallartaartwalk.com.

You can also see an intriguing collection of Mexican and international art at the Peter Gray Museum (www.cuc.udg.mx/?q=museo-de-arte-peter-gray) at the local university, Centro Universidad de la Costa (CUC), just north of the airport. Prominent artists on display include Joan Miro, Beatriz Castaneda, Carlos Merida, Jose Luis Cuevas, Pedro Coronel, and Pedro Friedeberg.

Finally, if you are looking to purchase art, you might find these galleries interesting.

**Galerie Des Artistes** (Leona Vicario 246, Centro | (322) 223-0006 | 11am–9pm Tue–Fri; 11am–2pm Sat).
This gallery features a variety of local artists, including Evelyne Boren, a favorite of ours. She has a life story as bright and vibrant as her paintings, working as an aquatic stunt double in James Bond films before becoming a full-time artist in the early 1960s. She is now internationally recognized, with personal galleries in Sante Fe, New Mexico and Sayulita. The gallery is associated with the gourmet restaurant, Café Des Artistes, directly across the street.

**Art Gallery Millan** (Amapas 129-1, Emiliano Zapata, Centro | (322) 137-3519 | 10am–8pm daily).
This gallery offers a variety of great works, including oil paintings by Eduardo Eguía and sculptures by Benito Arciniegas. Many pieces are not short of humor, not least the ceramic cyclist statuettes by Rodo Padilla. It's not far from Los Muertos Pier, or from our villa, *Casa Dos Cisnes*.

**Galería Pacífico** (Calle Aldama 174, 2nd fl., Centro | (322) 222-1982 | 10:30am–8pm Mon–Sat | www.galeriapacifico.com).

Pacífico features works by several leading artists, not least sculptor Ramiz Barquet, whose *Nostalgia* can be seen on the Malecón. It enjoys a high reputation. So much so, it's visited only by appointment during the summer.

**Galerias Sergio Bustamante** (Av. Juárez 275 Calle Corona, Centro | (322) 223-1405 | 11am–7pm Mon–Fri | www.sergiobustamante.com.mx).
Creator of life-size brass and ceramic works, Sergio Bustamante is known throughout the world for his quirky creations. His gallery produces a range of pieces most of which are priced in the thousands, but also well-priced purses, shoes, and jewelry.

**Basilio Badillo** also has a number of interesting venues including the Dante and Contempo galleries.

SHOPPING MALLS
If you need some clothing or forgot to pack something, there are two high-end, department store-type malls that have high quality offerings.

**Galerías Vallarta** (Av. Francisco Medina Ascencio No.2920, Col. Educación | (322) 209-0923 | 11am–9pm daily | www.galerias.com/GaleriasVallarta).
This is the main shopping mall, sited between the Zona Hotelera and Marina Vallarta overlooking the port. It has pretty much everything you'd need, with 91 brand stores inside. As you would expect, there are also restaurants, cafés, and a fast-food court, with a 12-theater cinema, too.

**La Isla** (Boulevard Francisco Medina Ascencio | (322) 688-1453 | 11am–11pm daily |
www.laislapuertovallarta.mx/en/home).
La Isla is the newest shopping center and is a beautiful outdoor mall, set off Highway 200 in the Zona Hotelera. Several stores sell souvenirs, but there are also higher end boutiques like Tommy Hilfiger, Benetton, Calvin Klein, and Guess. It's loved for its atmosphere, with a koi pond, turtle pond, and several fountains, but there is also a luxury VIP multiplex cinema with reclining chairs and food service, so lots to entertain you if it rains!

For more everyday items and supplies, there are some familiar US stores and supermarket chains in Puerto Vallarta.

**Walmart** (Av. Francisco Villa 1526, Vida Vallarta | (322) 224-9072 | 7am–11pm daily | www.walmart.com.mx).

**Costco** (Av Fluvial Vallarta 134 | (322) 226-2580 | 9am–9pm Mon–Sat; 9am–8pm Sun| www.costco.com.mx).

**Officemax** (Av Francisco Medina Ascencio 1800, Las Glorias | 1-800-713-7078 | 8am–9pm Mon–Fri; 9am–9pm Sat & Sun | www.officemax.com.mx).

**Home Depot** (Tepic 5348, Col. Las Juntas | (322) 226-5500 | 7am–10pm Mon–Sat; 8am–10pm Sun | homedepot.com.mx).

**La Comer** (Av Fluvial Vallarta - right next to Costco | (800) 377-7333 | 7am–11pm daily | www.lacomer.com.mx).
This gleaming, new hypermarket opened shortly before going to press, but we stopped by at the grand opening and it's amazing. They have an extraordinary selection of products for one-stop shopping, offering everything from Mexican baked goods and imported cheeses, wines, and foods, to washing machines, refrigerators, and motor scooters. A Walmart on steroids. We often mourn the loss of Puerto Vallarta's "sleepy, fishing-village feel," but having an expanded choice of these types of products is a luxury we appreciate and was unthinkable even 10 years ago.

# Good to Know

## Health

If you've been to Mexico before, you'll already know about the problems the food and water here can cause. Generally speaking, PV has a good reputation for the quality of its food, but it's important to be aware of the risks and what to avoid.

The most common condition is referred to as *turista* ("traveler's diarrhea"), caused by contaminated fruit, vegetables, or water. So, steer clear of any suspicious street food stands (we tend to avoid them altogether; there's really not a good reason to eat at them in the first place). Raw fish dishes, like *ceviche*, are delicious and always tempting, but we find it's a good idea to err on the side of caution and only order this at reputable restaurants.

It's best to drink bottled water. Look for *Agua Mineral* (mineral water), *Agua con Gas* (carbonated water) or *Agua Purificada* (purified water). At the restaurants we have recommended here, we always just order *agua de la casa* (house water) as they all use large purified water bottles to fill their pitchers.

Most villas are like ours (but check first) and have a UV water purification system installed enabling you to drink water from the tap throughout the house; in addition, our chef soaks all fruits and vegetables in an anti-bacterial solution using either Microdyn or Bacdyn. Cathryn has an extremely sensitive stomach and gets sick just by walking past street food and she never has had a problem from the water at our villa or in the recommended restaurants.

If you've already fallen victim, drink chamomile tea, which is available everywhere. You should also rehydrate yourself with a salt-sugar solution (½ teaspoon of salt & 4 tablespoons of sugar per quart of water) or an electrolyte enhanced drink available in different flavors at most pharmacies.

Pharmacies are plentiful and will carry Pepto Bismol, seltzer, and other remedies. Despite all of our precautions, we do occasionally fall victim to *turista*. When we do, we go to the pharmacy and buy Loperamida (it's the active ingredient in Imodium) for the diarrhea and *Butilhioscina/Metamizol sódico* (antispasmodic for the stomach and intestinal tract) to reduce stomach cramps and nausea. (DISCLAIMER: We are not doctors and don't pretend to be. Consult the pharmacist first before buying anything or taking anything. They are well-trained and informed. We're just giving you some suggestions based on our personal experience and as a point of reference).

Be aware that pharmacies in Mexico are different from US pharmacies (sorry Canadians… we've no experience with Canadian pharmacies so don't know how they compare) and are more like the European pharmacies with all over-the-counter medicines behind the counter. Even items like Pepto Bismol and Advil are only available at pharmacies (or at the pharmacy in one of the large *supermercados*) and you have to talk to someone to get said medicine.
So, forget about discreetly grabbing diarrhea medication and heading to the checkout. Instead, you will have to describe your symptoms to the pharmacist in front of eight new friends waiting for service behind you and watch the pharmacist get what you need from behind the counter. Although you might initially find this embarrassing, you undoubtedly won't be the first person they've seen that day with the issue and this procedure is totally normal.

In any case, if your problem persists for more than two days, see a doctor.

## Medical Care

Puerto Vallarta's newer hospitals are very well equipped and have a good selection of specialist staff, like Vallarta Medical Center in the Zona Hotelera, or Hospital CMQ, south of the Río Cuale.

## Medical Insurance

It's important to note here that foreign, non-Mexican insurance is NEVER accepted anywhere in Puerto Vallarta for any outpatient treatment. This includes consultations, medications, emergency room visits, diagnostic studies, physical therapy, etc. All fees must be paid out of pocket and can then be submitted to your insurance company for reimbursement.

For admissions to any private hospital, you will be requested to make a deposit at the time of admission, regardless of the type of insurance you have. This is kind of like opening a "bar tab" there. If you have insurance (foreign—in this case meaning non-Mexican-or otherwise), you must give your insurance information to the admissions department at that time. They will then contact your insurance company to obtain a Guarantee of Payment from your insurer in a timely manner. The patient is responsible for any co-pay and/or deductible. The amount of the deposit will depend on the severity of the admission.

Friends of ours have informed us that ACA ("Obamacare") insurance and Medicare do not pay anything outside of the United States but that most Medicare supplemental insurance ("Medi-Gap policies") will reimburse at 80% minus a US$200–US$250 co-payment.

**Doctors**

Some English-speaking doctors that either we know of personally or friends of ours have recommended from their personal use are:

**Dra. Guadalupe Lewgot** (Cardiologist-Internist) located in Medasist Hospital (see address below), her direct telephone number is: (322) 223-0444.

**Dra. Leslie Swindle** (Cardiologist & Internist) - her principal office is on the 3rd floor of CMQ Premier (see address below). Office number: (322) 221-1088 | Mobile Number: 044 (322) 294-0524.

**Dr. Adolfo Curiel** (Cardiologist) - located in Clinica Innova at Jacarandas #273. Office number: (322) 222-1889.

**Dr. Peter F. Gordon** (General Medicine) - his office is in the Vallarta Medical Center (see address below). Direct office number: (322) 293-1552 / 1553 | Mobile number: 044 (322) 205-7154.

If you'd prefer an American-trained doctor, Dr. Alfonso Rodríguez (located in the Intermedica Group building at Lucerna 148, (322) 293-1991) is a member of the International Association for Medical Assistance to Travelers (IAMAT).

US-expatriate Pamela Thompson operates a healthcare referral network and can put you in contact with any doctor or specialist you need through her firm, HealthCare Resources Puerto Vallarta (https://healthcareresourcespv.com. Telephone Office: (322) 222-9638) and Mobile: 044 (322) 107-7007. E-mail: Pamela@healthcareresourcespv.com). We have used her in the past and she was very responsive and helpful.

## Hospitals

For emergency care, Puerto Vallarta has five hospitals (one in two locations) that offer 24-hour services:

**Vallarta Medical Center**
(www.vallartamedicalcenter.mx) Los Tules 136, behind Plaza Caracol | (322) 178-3000
**Hospital CMQ** (Centro Médico Quirúrgico), with two locations: Basilio Badillo 365, between Av. Insurgentes and Aguacate | (322) 223-1919 | Emergency Number: (322) 223-0878 and Hospital CMQ Premiere located at Av. Francisco Villa 1749 | Reception: (322) 226-6500| Emergency Number: 044 (322) 779-9852).

**Hospiten Puerto Vallarta** (Blv. F. M. Ascencio 3970, outside of the marina | Switchboard (322) 226-2080 | To make appointments (322) 226-2062). NOTE: We have been told by someone in whom we have confidence that the prices charged here are unreasonably high. We have no personal knowledge of this however, but if you seek medical care here, and feel you are being unreasonably charged, you should report your experience to your consulate (see contact details listed further below).

**Medasist** (south of Río Cuale at Dieguez 360 | (322) 223-0656).

**San Javier** (Blv. F. M. Ascencio 2760, near the marina | (322) 226-1010).

## Emergency Ambulances

To call an emergency ambulance service, 24-hours:

**A C Health Ambulance Service**: (322) 299-2000 and (322) 209-1123

**IMR Ambulance Service** with bases in Sayulita, San Javier Riviera, Hospital San Javier Marina and Vallarta Medical Center: (322) 111-0231

## Pharmacies

If you are on medication, the good news is that you can bring it into the country, but only a limited amount and with a written prescription from your doctor. The US Embassy (mx.usembassy.gov/information-regarding-bringing-medications-into-mexico) has information on what is legal and illegal to import into Mexico. As in the US or Canada, if you need more medicine, you'll need to visit a pharmacy, but here are some points to consider.

While you'll find many of the US brands here, you won't find them all (sleep aids, for example). Many medications are marketed under different brands outside the United States, but you can generally find the local brand name online. In any case, the pharmacist will be able to help you with this.

Prescriptions for antibiotics or narcotics must be issued by a Mexican doctor to be legal, but they can be gotten fairly easily and inexpensively from a local doctor and many pharmacies have a doctor available for consultation right then and there without a previous appointment. The only thing more surprising than that is the unusually low price you will pay for the consultation and the medication. That being said, there are a number of smaller pharmacies that sell all kinds of prescription drugs, both US branded and generic, without any prescription. All of the major chains, like Farmacia Guadalajara, require prescriptions so don't try to haggle your way to a refill without a prescription… they won't do it. We know because we've tried. :) Overall, we recommend that you stick with the major pharmacy stores as the smaller, unbranded stores often offer medications of inconsistent quality and strength.

Pharmacies in PV usually open at 9am and close at 10pm (earlier on Sundays). Farmacias Guadalajara is a common chain and is open 24-hours. The nearest to us is at Insurgentes 261 (322) 222-0101), in the Zona Romántica, a couple of blocks south of Río Cuale but there are several more in the Banderas Bay area which you can find online.

**Emergency Contacts**

If you find yourself in an emergency situation and are a US or Canadian citizen, there is both a US Consulate and Canadian Consulate in the city. Both are close to the airport, with the Canadian office located in the Hotelera Zona and the US office located further north, in Nuevo Vallarta.

In an emergency after hours, you'll need to call the US Consul General in Guadalajara. If you are Canadian, you'll have to call the Canadian Embassy in Mexico City.

**United States Consulate** (Centro Plaza Comercial Paradise, Paseo de Cocoteros 85 Sur, 2nd fl., Nuevo Vallarta | (322) 222-0069/(333) 268-2145 (24-hrs) | 8:30am–12:30pm Mon–Thu).

**US Embassy** (Paseo de la Reforma 305, Col. Cuauhtémoc, Mexico City | (55) 5080-2000 | mx.usembassy.gov).

**US Consul General** (Progreso 175, Americana, 44100 Guadalajara | (333) 268-2100/268-2200 | mx.usembassy.gov).

**US Overseas Citizens Services** (888) 407-4747/(202) 501-4444 | www.travel.state.gov.

**Canadian Honorary Consul** (Plaza Peninsula, Local Sub F, Blv. F. M. Ascencio 2485 | (322) 293-0098/293-0099 | 9am–1pm Mon–Fri).

**Canadian Embassy** (Schiller 529, Miguel Hidalgo, Polanco, 11560 México City | 01-800-706-2900 | 9am–5pm Mon–Fri | www.travel.gc.ca/travelling).

**General Emergencies:**

**Emergency Number** – 911
**Police Dept.** – 911
**Fire Dept.** – tel. 322/224-7701

## Electricity

Mexico operates on the same 60-cycle, 120-volt system used in the rest of North America, so you don't need a converter. But because many Mexican outlets don't yet accommodate three-prong and polarized plugs, bringing your own 3-to-2 prong adapter is a good idea. There can be infrequent brownouts and blackouts, especially during the rainy season (but not at our villa because we have our own electrical substation!), so we recommend you also bring a surge protector. A universal adapter is probably the best option.

## Time Zone

Puerto Vallarta, Guadalajara, and the rest of Jalisco State fall into Central Standard Time (UTC -6), the same as Mexico City. Nayarit State is on Mountain Standard Time (UTC -7), but the coastal towns (Nuevo Vallarta, Bucerías, Punta de Mita, and along the Riviera Nayarit) changed to the same time zone as Puerto Vallarta some years ago to save tourists any confusion. Bear in mind that Mexico does observe daylight saving time, but not on the same schedule as the US.

## Tipping

At restaurants in Puerto Vallarta, tipping is now customary. The standard Mexican tip for good service is 10%, but when you're very happy then 15%–20% is usual.

When renting a villa with staff, the usual tip for full-time household staff is around 10% of the cost of the villa rental for good service and you should give more if you feel the staff went over and above your expectations. You normally don't tip the property manager.

Taxis are not usually tipped.

# Conclusion

We hope that *Puerto Vallarta Insider* helps you to enjoy the perfect vacation in this tropical paradise we call "home." And once you feel like a "local" too, we'd love to hear your ideas for additional entries into *Puerto Vallarta Insider*. Please send your ideas and comments to: PVInsider@PVInsiderBook.com.

And should you like to know more about our home, *Casa Dos Cisnes*, you can view a video and photo gallery of the home at www.pvluxuryvilla.com. We designed and built the home with love over ten years and now live there part-time over the course of each year, renting the villa out as a luxury vacation home when we're working or traveling elsewhere.

Additional information regarding the home's construction and architectural details are described and displayed in the book, *Casa Dos Cisnes, A Colonial Mexican Home Re-Imagined for Modern Living*, available for purchase here (www.amazon.com/Casa-Dos-Cisnes-Colonial-Reimagined-ebook/dp/B07L7G8MDG/) in Kindle and print versions.

We look forward to hearing about your experiences in this magical land called Mexico. ¡*Hasta pronto*!

Made in the USA
Coppell, TX
16 December 2019